POPE JOHN PAUL II

Pope John Paul II

In My Own Words

Compiled and edited by Anthony F. Chiffolo

Hodder & Stoughton
LONDON SYDNEY AUCKLAND

The editor and publisher gratefully acknowledge
permission to reprint / reproduce copyrighted works
granted by the publishers / sources listed on pages
114 – 15.

First published in Great Britain 1998,
by arrangement with Liguori Publications,
Liguori, Missouri, USA.

10 9 8 7 6 5 4 3 2 1

British Library Cataloguing in Publication Data
A record for this book is available from the British Library

ISBN 0 340 72240 1

Printed and bound in Great Britain by
Clays Ltd, St Ives plc

Hodder and Stoughton Ltd
A Division of Hodder Headline PLC
338 Euston Road
London NW1 3BH

Friends: I greet you and

all those dear to you,

I bless you and

I encourage you not to

grow faint as you travel

the right road.

Greeting, South Bronx, 1979

CONTENTS

INTRODUCTION IX

GOD THE FATHER, SON, AND HOLY SPIRIT ... 1

PRAYER 11

FAITH, HOPE, AND LOVE 17

SALVATION 25

TRUTH AND FREEDOM 31

THE CHRISTIAN LIFE 39

THE SANCTITY OF LIFE 55

MARRIAGE AND THE FAMILY 61

SOLIDARITY AND HUMAN RELATIONSHIPS... 67

PROGRESS AND THE MODERN WORLD 75

THE CHURCH 93

THE SACRAMENTS 99

THE PRIESTHOOD 105

MARY 109

PERMISSIONS AND ACKNOWLEDGMENTS 115

$\mathcal{I}$NTRODUCTION

Who among us has not been touched in some small way by Pope John Paul II, has not seen on television his celebration of the Mass or read in the newspapers his statements about various current issues or simply heard news of his travels? He is, perhaps, the most visible pope the Catholic Church has ever had. Wherever he appears, he is greeted with the adulation normally accorded pop stars or royalty. Perhaps this is because he is "The Pilgrim Pope," the most widely traveled pope in the history of the papacy. Speaking many different languages and motoring around in his "popemobile," he is the first to bring the pope's love to people across the globe. Indeed, he is the first pope ever to have visited a number of countries, including, recently, Cuba.

Born Karol Wojtyla on May 18, 1920, in Wadowice, Poland, Pope John Paul II studied literature and drama in Kraków. During the Nazi occupation he worked in a stone quarry and a chemical plant, and he also began studying secretly for the priesthood in 1942.

He was ordained in 1946 and then earned a doctorate in theology at the Angelicum in Rome.

Afterward, from 1948 to 1951, he served as a parish priest in Kraków, then spent a year studying philosophy at the Jagiellonian University. From 1952 to 1958 he taught social ethics at the Kraków seminary, and he also served as professor at the University of Lublin.

Consecrated auxiliary bishop in Kraków in 1958 and archbishop in 1964, Karol Wojtyla attended all four sessions of the Second Vatican Council. He is said to have written *Gaudium et Spes*, the Pastoral Constitution on the Church in the Modern World, and to have played a prominent role in the formulation of *Dignitatis Humanae*, the Declaration on Religious Liberty. And his apologetic of the traditional Catholic teaching about marriage, *Love and Responsibility*, inspired Pope Paul VI to rely extensively on Archbishop Wojtyla's counsel during the writing of *Humanae Vitae*. Following the council, Karol Wojtyla was appointed cardinal in 1967.

As bishop and then as cardinal in Kraków, Karol Wojtyla provided inspirational leadership to Polish Catholics during the atheistic Communist regime, championing human rights and humankind's need to seek and know God. His support of Solidarity and fervent opposition to Communism hastened its downfall in Europe.

Karol Wojtyla was elected pope on October 16, 1978—the first non-Italian pope in more than four hundred years. To emphasize his commitment to continue the reforms of the Second Vatican Council, he took the names of his predecessors: John, Paul, and John Paul. He is the 262d successor of Saint Peter.

As pope, John Paul II has traveled around the world to meet and teach and minister to millions of Catholics—in locations as diverse as cathedrals, baseball stadiums, schools, and soup kitchens. But Pope John Paul II is much more than a jet-setting celebrity. During the course of his papacy he has emerged as perhaps the world's most important moral leader, unafraid to testify to the truth in both word and deed. He has written myriad letters, addresses, and encyclicals to the bishops, priests, and faithful of the Church, emphasizing the sacredness of life, the splendor of truth, and the love of God, as the selections in this collection demonstrate. And he authorized the preparation of the *Catechism of the Catholic Church*, the first universal catechism to be issued in more than four hundred years, to make the doctrines of the Church known in modern terms to a worldwide audience.

But what makes Pope John Paul II such a beloved leader is the constancy of his example. He speaks what he knows to be true, whether he's saying Mass at Yankee Stadium or addressing the General Assembly at the United Nations. Wherever he travels, he takes time to pray—especially the rosary—and he shares his prayers with millions via television and radio, as well as videocassettes and audio recordings. Each place he has visited he has consecrated to the Blessed Virgin Mary. And he has demonstrated the true meaning of love, having forgiven the man who wounded him during an unsuccessful assassination attempt.

Thus when he asserts, "Jesus is a demanding friend," or explains, "Love is the gift of self," or advises, "Be faithful to your daily prayers," or exhorts, "Do not be afraid!" it is clear that his are not empty words, for they arise out of his lived experience. And trusting these admonitions, we come to trust the pope's greatest message, words so many find so hard to believe: "God loves you." It is this message, so eloquently and often expressed, that has enabled him to touch the hearts of millions.

—AFC

GOD THE FATHER, SON, AND HOLY SPIRIT

We must go to this Child, this Man,
the Son of God, at whatever inconvenience,
at whatever risk to ourselves, because to know
and love him will truly change our lives.

HOMILY AT CENTRAL PARK, 1995

"*Life*" is one of the most beautiful titles which the Bible attributes to God. He is the living God.

MESSAGE TO PONTIFICAL ACADEMY OF SCIENCES, 1996

God created man as rational and free, thereby placing Himself under man's judgment. *The history of salvation is also the history of man's continual judgment of God.* Not only of man's questions and doubts but of his actual judgment of God.

CROSSING THE THRESHOLD OF HOPE

Every time Christ exhorts us to have no fear, He has both God and man in mind. He means: *Do not be afraid of God,* who, according to philosophers, is the transcendent Absolute. Do not be afraid of God, but invoke Him with me: "Our Father" (Mt 6:9). *Do not be afraid to say "Father"!* Desire to be perfect just as He is, because He is perfect.

CROSSING THE THRESHOLD OF HOPE

God's love for us is freely given and unearned, surpassing all we could ever hope for or imagine. He does not love us because we have merited it or are worthy of it. God loves us, rather, because he is true to his own nature. As Saint John puts it, "God is love, and he who abides in love abides in God, and God in him" (1 Jn 4:16).

ADDRESS AT MISSION DOLORES, 1987

Christ offers you his friendship. He gave his life so that those who wish to answer his call can indeed become his friends. His is a friendship which is deep, genuine, loyal, and total, as all true friendship must be.

MESSAGE TO YOUNG PEOPLE, CAMAGÜEY, CUBA, 1998

We always feel unworthy of Christ's friendship. But it is a good thing that we should have a holy fear of not remaining faithful to it.

TO PRIESTS, 1988

It is Christ who made man's way his own, and who guides him, even when he is unaware of it.

CENTESIMUS ANNUS

The goal and target of our life is he, the Christ, who awaits us—each one singly and all together—to lead us across the boundaries of time to the eternal embrace of the God who loves us.

MESSAGE TO YOUNG PEOPLE,
WORLD YOUTH DAY, 1996

This poor Babe, for whom "there was no room in the inn," in spite of appearances, is the sole Heir of the whole of creation. He came to share with us this birthright of his, so that we, having become children of divine adoption, might have a part in the inheritance that he brought with him into the world.

"URBI ET ORBI," 1995

*W*hat really matters in life is that we are loved by Christ, and that we love him in return. In comparison to the love of Jesus, everything else is secondary. And without the love of Jesus, everything else is useless.

PRAYER AT ST. PETER'S, PHILADELPHIA, 1979

*T*here is no evil to be faced that Christ does not face with us. There is no enemy that Christ has not already conquered. There is no cross to bear that Christ has not already borne for us, and does not now bear with us.

HOMILY IN ORIOLES PARK AT CAMDEN YARDS, 1995

*C*hrist himself carried a burden, and his burden—the cross—was made heavier by the sins of us all. But Christ did not avoid the cross; he accepted it and carried it willingly. Moreover, he now stands beside those weighed down by trials and persecutions, remaining beside them to the end. It is for all people and with all people that he carries the cross to Calvary, and it is there that for all of us he is nailed to his cross. He dies the death of a criminal, the most humiliating death known to the world at that time. That is why to those in our own century who carry terrible burdens he is able to say: "Come to me! I am your Brother in suffering. There is no humiliation or bitterness which I do not know!"

HOMILY AT AQUEDUCT RACETRACK, 1995

*J*esus Christ has taken the lead on the way of the cross. He has suffered first. He does not drive us toward suffering but shares it with us, wanting us to have life and to have it in abundance.

MEETING WITH THE SICK AND SUFFERING, 1998

*T*he name of Jesus, like the Word of God that he is, is a two-edged sword. It is a name that means salvation and life; it is a name that means a struggle and a cross, just as it did for him. But it is also the name in which we find strength to proclaim and live the truth of the Gospel: not with arrogance, but with confident joy; not with self-righteousness, but with humble repentance before God; never with enmity and always with charity.

ADDRESS AT LOS ANGELES, 1987

The splendor of Christ's glory is reflected in the face of every human being, and is even more so when that face is emaciated by hunger, saddened by exile, or oppressed by poverty and misery.

Catholic Relief Services Message, 1995

The Incarnation of the Son of God attests that God goes in search of man. Jesus speaks of this search as the finding of a lost sheep. It is a search which begins in the heart of God....If God goes in search of man, created in his own image and likeness, he does so because he loves him eternally in the Word, and wishes to raise him in Christ to the dignity of an adoptive son. God therefore goes in search of man who is his special possession in a way unlike any other creature.

Tertio Millennio Adveniente

With man—with each man without any exception whatever—Christ is in a way united, even when man is unaware of it.

Redemptor Hominis

*M*aterialistic concerns and one-sided values are never sufficient to fill the heart and mind of a human person. A life reduced to the sole dimension of possessions, of consumer goods, of temporal concerns will never let you discover and enjoy the full richness of your humanity. It is only in God—in Jesus, God made man—that you will fully understand what you are. He will unveil to you the true greatness of yourselves: that you are redeemed by him and taken up in his love; that you are made truly free in him who said about himself: "If the Son frees you, you will be free indeed" (Jn 8:36).

MESSAGE TO STUDENTS,
THE CATHOLIC UNIVERSITY, 1979

*T*he Spirit instills in us a desire for the world to come, but he also inspires, purifies, and strengthens those noble longings by which we strive to make earthly life more human.

HOMILY AT AQUEDUCT RACETRACK, 1995

$\mathcal{T}$he Holy Spirit is given to the Church as the source of strength to conquer sin. Only God has the power to forgive sins, because he alone sees right into the human person and can measure human responsibility completely. Sin remains, in its psychological depth, a secret which God alone has the power to enter, in order to say to a person the efficacious words: "Your sins are forgiven you, you are pardoned."

MASS WITH YOUTH,
HRADEC KRÁLOVÉ, CZECH REPUBLIC, 1997

$\mathcal{T}$he modern technological world can offer us many pleasures, many comforts of life. It can even offer us temporary escapes from life. But what the world can never offer is lasting joy and peace. These are the gifts which only the Holy Spirit can give.

MEETING WITH YOUTH,
NEW ORLEANS, 1987

$\mathcal{M}$ay the Holy Spirit,
The Spirit of Pentecost,
help you to clarify what is ambiguous,
to give warmth to what is indifferent,
to enlighten what is obscure,
to be before the world true and generous
witnesses of Christ's love,
for "no one can live without love."

PRAYER AT INSTITUTE CATHOLIQUE, PARIS, 1980

$\mathcal{P}$RAYER

If you follow Jesus' advice and pray to God constantly, then you will learn to pray well. God himself will teach you.

MEETING WITH YOUTH, NEW ORLEANS, 1987

What is prayer? It is commonly held to be a conversation. In a conversation there are always an "I" and a "thou" or "you." In this case the "Thou" is with a capital T. If at first the "I" seems to be the most important element in prayer, prayer teaches that the situation is actually different. *The "Thou" is more important, because our prayer begins with God.*

CROSSING THE THRESHOLD OF HOPE

We begin to pray, believing that it is our own initiative that compels us to do so. Instead, we learn that it is always God's initiative within us....

CROSSING THE THRESHOLD OF HOPE

It is a beautiful and salutary thought that, wherever people are praying in the world, there the Holy Spirit is, the living breath of prayer. It is a beautiful and salutary thought to recognize that, if prayer is offered throughout the world, in the past, in the present and in the future, equally widespread is the presence and action of the Holy Spirit, who "breathes" prayer in the heart of man in all the endless range of the most varied situations and conditions.

DOMINUM ET VIVIFICANTEM

*T*he Holy Spirit is the gift that comes into man's heart together with prayer. In prayer he manifests himself first of all and above all as the gift that "helps us in our weakness." This is the magnificent thought developed by Saint Paul in the Letter to the Romans, when he writes: "For we do not know how to pray as we ought, but the Spirit himself intercedes for us with sighs too deep for words" (8:26). Therefore, the Holy Spirit not only enables us to pray, but guides us "from within" in prayer: he is present in our prayer and gives it a divine dimension.

DOMINUM ET VIVIFICANTEM

*M*any times, through the influence of the Spirit, prayer rises from the human heart in spite of prohibitions and persecutions and even official proclamations....Prayer always remains the voice of all those who apparently have no voice....

DOMINUM ET VIVIFICANTEM

$\mathcal{P}$rayer...brings the saving power of Jesus Christ into the decisions and actions of everyday life.

GREETING IN ST. PATRICK'S CATHEDRAL, 1995

$\mathcal{B}$e faithful to your daily prayers; they will keep your faith alive and vibrant.

MESSAGE TO SEMINARIANS, CHICAGO, 1979

$\mathcal{C}$hrist remains primary in your life only when he enjoys the first place in your mind and heart. Thus you must continuously unite yourself to him in prayer....Without prayer there can be no joy, no hope, no peace. For prayer is what keeps us in touch with Christ.

MESSAGE TO RELIGIOUS WOMEN, WASHINGTON, D.C., 1979

$\mathcal{W}$hat enormous power the prayer of children has! This becomes a model for grownups themselves: praying with simple and complete trust means praying as children pray.

LETTER OF THE POPE TO THE CHILDREN IN THE YEAR OF THE FAMILY

$\mathcal{I}$f you really wish to follow Christ, if you want your love for him to grow and last, then you must be faithful to prayer. It is the key to the vitality of your life in Christ. Without prayer, your faith and love will die. If you are constant in daily prayer and in the Sunday celebration of Mass, your love for Jesus will increase. And your heart will know deep joy and peace, such as the world could never give.

MEETING WITH YOUTH, NEW ORLEANS, 1987

$\mathcal{P}$rayer can truly change your life. For it turns your attention away from yourself and directs your mind and your heart toward the Lord. If we look only at ourselves, with our own limitations and sins, we quickly give way to sadness and discouragement. But if we keep our eyes fixed on the Lord, then our hearts are filled with hope, our minds are washed in the light of truth, and we come to know the fullness of the Gospel with all its promise and life.

MEETING WITH YOUTH, NEW ORLEANS, 1987

*O*nly the human person, created in the image and likeness of God, is capable of raising a hymn of praise and thanksgiving to the Creator. The Earth, with all its creatures, and the entire universe call on man to be their voice.

HOMILY AT SAN ANTONIO, 1987

FAITH, HOPE, AND LOVE

People cannot live without love.
They are called to love God
and their neighbor, but in order
to love properly they must be certain
that God loves them.
God loves you, dear children!
This is what I want to tell you. . . .

LETTER OF THE POPE TO THE CHILDREN
IN THE YEAR OF THE FAMILY

$\mathcal{I}$n the very search for faith an implicit faith is already present, and therefore the necessary condition for salvation is already satisfied.

CROSSING THE THRESHOLD OF HOPE

$\mathcal{F}$aith is always demanding, because faith leads us beyond ourselves. It leads us directly to God. Faith also imparts a vision of life's purpose and stimulates us to action....Christ has commanded us to let the light of the Gospel shine forth in our service to society. How can we profess faith in God's word, and then refuse to let it inspire and direct our thinking, our activity, our decisions, and our responsibilities toward one another?

HOMILY IN ORIOLES PARK AT CAMDEN YARDS, 1995

$\mathcal{B}$y the practice of your religion you are called to give witness to your faith. And because actions speak louder than words, you are called to proclaim, by the conduct of your daily lives, that you really do believe that Jesus Christ is Lord!

MESSAGE TO HIGH SCHOOL STUDENTS,
MADISON SQUARE GARDEN, 1979

*W*ithout faith in God, there can be no hope, no lasting, authentic hope. To stop believing in God is to start down a path that can lead only to emptiness and despair.

YOUTH TELECONFERENCE, LOS ANGELES, 1987

*T*o evangelize is to give an account to all of the hope that is in us.

MESSAGE FOR WORLD MIGRATION DAY, 1997

*W*e cannot live without hope. We have to have some purpose in life, some meaning to our existence. We have to aspire to something. Without hope, we begin to die.

YOUTH TELECONFERENCE, LOS ANGELES, 1987

*H*ope comes from God, from our belief in God. People of hope are those who believe God created them for a purpose and that he will provide for their needs.

YOUTH TELECONFERENCE, LOS ANGELES, 1987

*T*o become like a little child—with complete trust in the Father and with the meekness taught by the Gospel—is not only an ethical imperative; it is a reason for hope. Even where the difficulties are so great as to lead to discouragement and the power of evil so overwhelming as to dishearten, those who can rediscover the simplicity of a child can begin to hope anew.

MESSAGE FOR WORLD DAY OF PEACE, 1996

*I*n our bodies we are a mere speck in the vast created universe, but by virtue of our souls we transcend the whole material world. I invite you to reflect on what makes each one of you truly marvelous and unique. Only a human being like you can think and speak and share your thoughts in different languages with other human beings all over the world, and through that language express the beauty of art and poetry and music and literature and the theater, and so many other uniquely human accomplishments.

And most important of all, only God's precious human beings are capable of loving.

HOMILY AT CENTRAL PARK, 1995

*L*ove can overcome great obstacles, and God's love can totally transform the world.

MEETING WITH CHARITIES,
SAN ANTONIO, 1987

*I*nner peace comes from knowing that one is loved by God and from the desire to respond to his love.

"WOMEN: TEACHERS OF PEACE," 1995.

*G*enuine love…is demanding. But its beauty lies precisely in the demands it makes. Only those able to make demands on themselves in the name of love can then demand love from others.

MESSAGE TO YOUNG PEOPLE,
CAMAGÜEY, CUBA, 1998

*L*ove is the gift of self. It means emptying oneself to reach out to others. In a certain sense, it means forgetting oneself for the good of others.

"TRUE HUMAN LOVE REFLECTS THE DIVINE," 1993

$\mathcal{L}$ove is the force that opens hearts to the word of Jesus and to his Redemption: love is the only basis for human relationships that respect in one another the dignity of the children of God created in his image and saved by the death and Resurrection of Jesus; love is the only driving force that impels us to share with our brothers and sisters all that we are and have.

HOMILY AT GRANT PARK, CHICAGO, 1979

$\mathcal{W}$e cannot live without love. If we do not encounter love, if we do not experience it and make it our own, and if we do not participate intimately in it, our life is meaningless. Without love we remain incomprehensible to ourselves.

MESSAGE TO RELIGIOUS WOMEN,
WASHINGTON, D.C., 1979

*L*ife is a talent entrusted to us so that we can transform it and increase it, making it a gift to others. No man is an iceberg drifting on the ocean of history. Each one of us belongs to a great family, in which he has his own place and his own role to play. Selfishness makes people deaf and dumb; love opens eyes and hearts, enabling people to make that original and irreplaceable contribution which, together with the thousands of deeds of so many brothers and sisters, often distant and unknown, converges to form the mosaic of charity which can change the tide of history.

MESSAGE FOR WORLD YOUTH DAY, 1996

SALVATION

Ultimately, only God can save man, but He expects man to cooperate. The fact that man can cooperate with God determines his authentic greatness. The truth according to which man is called to cooperate with God in all things, with a view toward the ultimate purpose of his life—his salvation and divinization—found expression in the Eastern tradition in the doctrine of synergism. With God, man "creates" the world; with God, man "creates" his personal salvation. The divinization of man comes from God. But here, too, man must cooperate with God.

CROSSING THE THRESHOLD OF HOPE

$\mathcal{A}$wareness of our own sinfulness, including that which is inherited, is the first condition for salvation; the next is the confession of this sin before God, who desires only to receive this confession so that He can save man. *To save means to embrace and lift up with redemptive love*, with love that is *always greater* than any sin.

CROSSING THE THRESHOLD OF HOPE

$\mathcal{N}$o human sin can erase the mercy of God, or prevent him from unleashing all his triumphant power, if we only call upon him.

VERITATIS SPLENDOR

$\mathcal{T}$he power of Christ's Cross and Resurrection is greater than any evil which man could or should fear.

CROSSING THE THRESHOLD OF HOPE

$\mathcal{T}$he precepts of the Lord are a gift of grace entrusted to man always and solely for his good, for the preservation of his personal dignity and the pursuit of his happiness.

EVANGELIUM VITAE

Through Christ's sacrifice on the Cross, the victory of the Kingdom of God has been achieved once and for all. Nevertheless, the Christian life involves a struggle against temptation and the forces of evil. Only at the end of history will the Lord return in glory for the final judgment with the establishment of a new heaven and a new earth; but as long as time lasts, the struggle between good and evil continues even in the human heart itself.

CENTESIMUS ANNUS

The true and proper meaning of mercy does not consist only in looking, however penetratingly and compassionately, at moral, physical or material evil: mercy is manifested in its true and proper aspect when it restores to value, promotes and draws good from all the forms of evil existing in the world and in man.

DIVES IN MISERICORDIA

An act of merciful love is only really such when we are deeply convinced at the moment that we perform it that we are at the same time receiving mercy from the people who are accepting it from us. If this bilateral and reciprocal quality is absent, our actions are not yet true acts of mercy, nor has there yet been fully completed in us that conversion to which Christ has show us the way by his words and example, even to the Cross, nor are we yet sharing fully in the magnificent source of merciful love that has been revealed to us by him.

DIVES IN MISERICORDIA

*C*hrist, in revealing the love-mercy of God, at the same time demanded from people that they also should be guided in their lives by love and mercy. This requirement forms part of the very essence of the messianic message, and constitutes the heart of the Gospel *ethos*.

DIVES IN MISERICORDIA

*F*orgiveness demonstrates the presence in the world of the love which is more powerful than sin. Forgiveness is also the fundamental condition for reconciliation, not only in the relationship of God with man, but also in relationships between people. A world from which forgiveness was eliminated would be nothing but a world of cold and unfeeling justice, in the name of which each person would claim his or her own rights vis-à-vis others....

DIVES IN MISERICORDIA

$\mathcal{M}$ercy in itself, as a perfection of the infinite God, is also infinite. Also infinite therefore and inexhaustible is the Father's readiness to receive the prodigal children who return to his home. Infinite are the readiness and power of forgiveness which flow continually from the marvelous value of the sacrifice of the Son. No human sin can prevail over this power or even limit it. On the part of man only a lack of good will can limit it, a lack of readiness to be converted and to repent, in other words persistence in obstinacy, opposing grace and truth, especially in the face of the witness of the Cross and Resurrection of Christ.

DIVES IN MISERICORDIA

*W*hen it comes to salvation in the kingdom of God, it is not a question of just wages, but of the undeserved generosity of God, who gives himself as the supreme gift to each and every person who shares in divine life through sanctifying grace.

HOMILY AT DETROIT, 1987

*E*ach of us is an individual, a person, a creature of God, one of his children, someone very special whom God loves and for whom Christ died. This identity of ours determines the way we must live, the way we must act, the way we must view our mission in the world. We come from God, we depend on God, God has a plan for us—a plan for our lives, for our bodies, for our souls, for our future. This plan for us is extremely important—so important that God became man to explain it to us.

MEETING WITH YOUTH, NEW ORLEANS, 1987

*T*RUTH AND FREEDOM

You cannot insist on the right to choose,
without also insisting on the duty to choose
well, the duty to choose the truth.

HOMILY AT COLUMBIA, SOUTH CAROLINA, 1987

$\mathscr{T}$he Gospel contains a *fundamental paradox*: to find life, one must lose life; to be born, one must die; to save oneself, one must take up the cross. This is the essential truth of the Gospel, which always and everywhere is bound to meet with man's protest.

Always and everywhere the Gospel will be a challenge to human weakness. But precisely in this challenge lies all its power. Man, perhaps subconsciously waits for such a challenge; *indeed, man feels the inner need to transcend himself*. Only in transcending himself does man become fully human....

CROSSING THE THRESHOLD OF HOPE

$\mathscr{M}$*an cannot be forced to accept the truth.* He can be drawn toward the truth only by his own nature, that is, by his own freedom, which commits him to search sincerely for truth and, when he finds it, to adhere to it both in his convictions and in his behavior.

CROSSING THE THRESHOLD OF HOPE

$\mathcal{I}$t is quite human for the sinner to acknowledge his weakness and to ask mercy for his failings; what is unacceptable is the attitude of one who makes his own weakness the criterion of the truth about the good, so that he can feel self-justified, without even the need to have recourse to God and his mercy.

VERITATIS SPLENDOR

$\mathcal{M}$an remains above all a being who seeks the truth and strives to live in that truth, deepening his understanding of it through a dialogue which involves past and future generations.

CENTESIMUS ANNUS

$\mathcal{J}$esus Christ meets the man of every age, including our own, with the same words: "You will know the truth, and the truth will make you free" (Jn 8:32). These words contain both a fundamental requirement and a warning: the requirement of an honest relationship with regard to truth as a condition for authentic freedom, and the warning to avoid every kind of illusory freedom, every superficial unilateral freedom, every freedom that fails to enter into the whole truth about man and the world.

REDEMPTOR HOMINIS

*B*ecause by its nature the content of faith is meant for all humanity, it must be translated into all cultures....The expression of truth can take different forms. The renewal of these forms of expression becomes necessary for the sake of transmitting to the people of today the Gospel message in its unchanging meaning.

ET UNUM SINT

*A*t the heart of every culture lies the attitude man takes to the greatest mystery: the mystery of God. Different cultures are basically different ways of facing the question of the meaning of personal existence.

CENTESIMUS ANNUS

*A*lthough each individual has a right to be respected in his own journey in search of the truth, there exists a prior moral obligation, and a grave one at that, to seek the truth and to adhere to it once it is known.

VERITATIS SPLENDOR

*R*evelation teaches that the power to decide what is good and what is evil does not belong to man, but to God alone. The man is certainly free, inasmuch as he can understand and accept God's commands. And he possesses an extremely far-reaching freedom, since he can eat "of every tree of the garden." But his freedom is not unlimited: it must halt before the "tree of the knowledge of good and evil," for it is called to accept the moral law given by God. In fact, human freedom finds its authentic and complete fulfillment precisely in the acceptance of that law. God, who alone is good, knows perfectly what is good for man, and by virtue of his very love proposes this good to man in the commandments.

VERITATIS SPLENDOR

$\mathcal{J}$esus' message applies to all the areas of life. He reveals to us the truth of our lives and all aspects of this truth. Jesus tells us that the purpose of our freedom is to say yes to God's plan for our lives. What makes our yes so important is that we say it freely; we are able to say no. Jesus teaches us that we are accountable to God, that we must follow our consciences, but that our consciences must be formed according to God's plan for our lives. In all our relationships to other people and to the world, Jesus teaches us what we must do, how we must live in order not to be deceived, in order to walk in truth.

MEETING WITH YOUTH, NEW ORLEANS, 1987

$\mathcal{B}$e faithful to the truth and to its transmission, for truth endures; truth will not go away. Truth will not pass or change.

MESSAGE TO U.N. JOURNALISTS, 1979

$\mathcal{N}$owadays it is sometimes held, though wrongly, that freedom is an end in itself, that each human being is free when he makes use of freedom as he wishes, and that this must be our aim in the lives of individuals and societies. In reality, freedom is a great gift only when we know how to use it consciously for everything that is our true good. Christ teaches us that the best use of freedom is charity, which takes concrete form in self-giving and in service.

REDEMPTOR HOMINIS

*F*reedom negates and destroys itself, and becomes a factor leading to the destruction of others, when it no longer recognizes and respects its essential link with the truth. When freedom, out of a desire to emancipate itself from all forms of tradition and authority, shuts out even the most obvious evidence of an objective and universal truth...then the person ends up by no longer taking as the sole and indisputable point of reference for his own choices the truth about good and evil, but only his subjective and changeable opinion or, indeed, his selfish interest and whim.

EVANGELIUM VITAE

*W*hile it is true that the taking of life not yet born or in its final stages is sometimes marked by a mistaken sense of altruism and human compassion, it cannot be denied that such a culture of death, taken as a whole, betrays a completely individualistic concept of freedom, which ends up by becoming the freedom of "the strong" against the weak who have no choice but to submit.

Evangelium Vitae

O Lord, bestow on your faithful the Spirit of truth and peace, that they may know you with all their soul, and generously carrying out what pleases you, may always enjoy your benefits.
Through Christ our Lord.
Amen.

General Audience, Rome, 1980

THE
CHRISTIAN LIFE

*The true success of our lives consists
in knowing and doing the will of Jesus,
in doing whatever Jesus tells us.*

MEETING WITH YOUTH, NEW ORLEANS, 1987

*E*veryone has a vocation: parents, teachers, students, workers, professional people, people who are retired. Everyone has something to do for God.

HOMILY AT GIANTS STADIUM, 1995

*T*he search and discovery of God's will for you is a deep and fascinating endeavor. It requires of you the attitude of trust expressed in the words of the Psalm…"you will show me the path to life, fullness of joy in your presence, the delights at your right hand forever" (16:11). Every vocation, every path to which Christ calls us, ultimately leads to fulfillment and happiness, because it leads to God, to sharing in God's own life.

MESSAGE TO YOUTH

*T*rue holiness does not mean a flight from the world; rather, it lies in the effort to incarnate the Gospel in everyday life, in the family, at school and at work, and in social and political involvement.

TO CATHOLIC CHARISMATICS, 1996

$\mathcal{G}$od can use our weakness as easily as our strength in order to accomplish his will.

MEETING WITH PRIESTS, MIAMI, 1987

$\mathcal{D}$o not be afraid! Life with Christ is a wonderful adventure. He alone can give full meaning to life, he alone is the center of history. Live by him!

MASS WITH YOUTH, HRADEC KRÁLOVÉ, CZECH REPUBLIC, 1997

$\mathcal{T}$he whole of the Christian life is like a great pilgrimage to the house of the Father, whose unconditional love for every human creature, and in particular for the "prodigal son," we discover anew each day. This pilgrimage takes place in the heart of each person, extends to the believing community and then reaches to the whole of humanity.

TERTIO MILLENNIO ADVENIENTE

Conversion to God always consists in discovering his mercy, that is, in discovering that love which is patient and kind as only the Creator and Father can be....Conversion to God is always the fruit of the "rediscovery" of this Father, who is rich in mercy.

Authentic knowledge of the God of mercy, the God of tender love, is a constant and inexhaustible source of conversion, not only as a momentary interior act but also as a permanent attitude, as a state of mind. Those who come to know God in this way, who "see" him in this way, can live only in a state of being continually converted to him.

Dives in Misericordia

The Gospel is certainly demanding. We know that Christ never permitted His disciples and those who listened to Him to entertain any illusions about this. On the contrary, He spared no effort in preparing them for every type of internal or external difficulty, always aware of the fact that they might well decide to abandon Him. Therefore, if He says, "Be not afraid!" He certainly does not say it in order to nullify in some way that which He has required. Rather, by these words He confirms the entire truth of the Gospel and all the demands it contains. At the same time, however, He reveals that *His demands never exceed man's abilities*. If man accepts these demands with an attitude of faith, he will also find in the grace that God never fails to give him the necessary strength to meet those demands.

CROSSING THE THRESHOLD OF HOPE

*T*he way Jesus shows you is not easy. Rather, it is like a path winding up a mountain. Do not lose heart! The steeper the road, the faster it rises toward ever wider horizons.

MESSAGE FOR WORLD YOUTH DAY, 1996

*I*t is true: Jesus is a demanding friend. He points to lofty goals: he asks us to go out of ourselves in order to meet him, entrusting to him our whole life: "Whoever loses his life for my sake and that of the gospel will save it" (Mk 8:35). The proposal may seem difficult, and, in some cases, frightening. But—I ask you—is it better to be resigned to a life without ideals, to a world made in our image and likeness, or rather, generously to seek truth, goodness, justice, working for a world that reflects the beauty of God, even at the cost of facing the trials it may involve?

MESSAGE FOR WORLD YOUTH DAY, 1996

$\mathscr{I}$n order to hold fast to the fundamental values which keep them sinless, Christians sometimes have to suffer marginalization and persecution—at times heroically—because of moral choices which are contrary to the world's behavior....This is the cost of Christian witness, of a worthy life in the eyes of God. If you are not willing to pay this price, your lives will be empty....

HOMILY AT CAMAGÜEY, CUBA, 1998

Christians, like all people of good will, are called upon under grave obligation of conscience not to cooperate formally in practices which, even if permitted by civil legislation, are contrary to God's law.

EVANGELIUM VITAE

*T*hose who live "by the flesh" experience God's Law as a burden, and indeed as a denial or at least a restriction of their own freedom. On the other hand, those who are impelled by love and "walk by the Spirit" (Gal 5:16), and who desire to serve others, find in God's Law the fundamental and necessary way in which to practice love as something freely chosen and freely lived out. Indeed, they feel an interior urge—a genuine "necessity" and no longer a form of coercion—not to stop at the minimum demands of the Law, but to live them in their "fullness."

VERITATIS SPLENDOR

*T*o imitate and live out the love of Christ is not possible for man by his own strength alone. He becomes capable of this love only by virtue of a gift received….Christ's gift is his Spirit….

VERITATIS SPLENDOR

*T*he Father puts in our hands the task of beginning to build here on earth the "kingdom of heaven" which the Son came to announce and which will find its fulfillment at the end of time.

It is our duty then to live in history, side by side with our peers, sharing their worries and hopes, because the Christian is and must be fully a man of his time. He cannot escape into another dimension, ignoring the tragedies of his era, closing his eyes and heart to the anguish that pervades life. On the contrary, it is he who, although not "of" this world, is immersed "in" this world every day, ready to hasten to wherever there is a brother in need of help, a tear to be dried, a request for help to be answered. On this will we be judged.

MESSAGE FOR WORLD YOUTH DAY, 1996

*I*n children there is something that must never be missing in people who want to enter the kingdom of heaven. People who are destined to go to heaven are simple like children, and like children are full of trust, rich in goodness and pure. Only people of this sort can find in God a Father and, thanks to Jesus, can become in their own turn children of God.

LETTER OF THE POPE TO THE CHILDREN
IN THE YEAR OF THE FAMILY

$\mathcal{P}$eace is a gift of God; but men and women must first accept this gift in order to build a peaceful world. People can do this only if they have a childlike simplicity of heart. This is one of the most profound and paradoxical aspects of the Christian message: to become childlike is more than just a moral requirement but a dimension of the mystery of the Incarnation itself.

The Son of God did not come in power and glory, as he will at the end of the world, but as a child, needy and poor. Fully sharing our human condition in all things but sin, he also took on the frailty and hope for the future which are part of being a child. After that decisive moment for the history of humanity, to despise childhood means to despise the One who showed the greatness of his love by humbling himself and forsaking all glory in order to redeem mankind.

MESSAGE FOR WORLD DAY OF PEACE, 1996

$\mathcal{B}$ut how are you to be recognized as true disciples of Christ? By the fact that you have "love for one another" (Jn 13:35) after the example of his love: a love that is freely given,

infinitely patient and denied to no one. Fidelity
to the new commandment will be the
guarantee that you are consistent with respect
to what you are proclaiming....In this world
you are called to live fraternally, not as a utopia
but as a real possibility; in this society you are
called, as true missionaries of Christ, to build
the civilization of love.

MESSAGE FOR WORLD YOUTH DAY, 1996

*Y*our great contribution to the
evangelization of your own society is made
through your lives. Christ's message must live
in you and in the way you live and in the way
you refuse to live....Your lives must spread the
fragrance of Christ's Gospel throughout the
world.

MEETING WITH LAITY, SAN FRANCISCO, 1987

*I*t is through the free gift of self that one
truly finds oneself. This gift is made possible by
the human person's essential "capacity for
transcendence."...As a person, he can give
himself to another person or to other persons,
and ultimately to God, who is the author of our

being and who alone can fully accept our gift. Man is alienated if he refuses to transcend himself and to live the experience of self-giving and of the formation of an authentic human community oriented toward his final destiny, which is God.

CENTESIMUS ANNUS

*N*ever forget that blindly following the impulse of our emotions often means becoming a slave to our passions.

MESSAGE TO YOUNG PEOPLE, CAMAGÜEY, CUBA, 1998

*T*here is no room in the world for selfishness. It destroys the meaning of life; it destroys the meaning of love; it reduces the human person to a subhuman level.

MEETING WITH YOUTH, NEW ORLEANS, 1987

*W*hat does it mean to remain sinless? It means living your life according to the moral principles of the Gospel which the Church sets before you.

HOMILY AT CAMAGÜEY, CUBA, 1998

*I*ndifference in the face of human suffering, passivity before the causes of pain in the world, cosmetic remedies which lead to no deep healing of persons and peoples: These are grave sins of omission, in the face of which every person of good will must be converted and listen to the cry of those who suffer.

MEETING WITH THE SICK AND SUFFERING, 1998

*C*hrist is very clear: When we ourselves are without sympathy or mercy, when we are guided by "blind" justice alone, then we cannot count on the mercy of that "Great Creditor" who is God—God, before whom we are all debtors.

HOMILY AT NEW ORLEANS, 1987

*C*hrist responds neither directly nor abstractly to human questioning about the meaning of suffering. Human beings come to know his saving response in so far as they share in the sufferings of Christ. The response which comes from this sharing is before all else a call. It is a vocation. Christ does not explain in some abstract way the reasons for suffering, but says first of all: "Follow me," "Come," with your suffering share in this work of salvation of the world, which is realized through my suffering, by means of my Cross.

SALVIFICI DOLORIS

*T*hose who suffer are no burden to others, but with their suffering contribute to the salvation of all.

MEETING WITH THE SICK AND SUFFERING, 1998

*T*he eloquence of the parable of the Good Samaritan, as of the entire Gospel, is in real terms this: Human beings must feel personally called to witness to love in the midst of suffering.

MEETING WITH THE SICK AND SUFFERING, 1998

*T*he distinctive mark of the Christian, today more than ever, must be love for the poor, the weak, the suffering. Living out this demanding commitment requires a total reversal of the alleged values which make people seek only their own good: power, pleasure, the unscrupulous accumulation of wealth. Yes, it is precisely to this radical conversion that Christ's disciples are called.

MESSAGE FOR WORLD DAY OF PEACE, 1998

$\mathcal{D}$o not be afraid, I say, because great courage is required if we are to open the doors to Christ, if we are to let Christ enter into our hearts so fully that we can say with Saint Paul, "The life I live now is not my own; Christ is living in me" (Gal 2:20)....You need courage to follow Christ, especially when you recognize that so much of our dominant culture is a culture of flight from God....

ADDRESS AT VESPERS, ST. JOSEPH'S SEMINARY, 1995

$\mathcal{B}$e generous in giving your life to the Lord. Do not be afraid! You have nothing to fear, because God is the Lord of history and of the universe. Let grow in you the desire for great and noble projects. Nourish a sense of solidarity: these are the signs of the divine action in your hearts. Place at the use of your communities the talents which Providence has lavished on you. The more ready you are to give yourselves to God and to others, the more you will discover the authentic meaning of life. God expects much of you!

MESSAGE FOR WORLD DAY OF PRAYER
FOR VOCATIONS, 1996

THE SANCTITY OF LIFE

Man is called to a fullness of life which far exceeds the dimensions of his earthly existence, because it consists in sharing the very life of God. The loftiness of this supernatural vocation reveals the greatness and the inestimable value of human life even in its temporal phase.

EVANGELIUM VITAE

The life which God gives man is quite different from the life of all other living creatures, inasmuch as man...is a manifestation of God in the world, a sign of his presence, a trace of his glory....Man has been given a sublime dignity, based on the intimate bond which unites him to his Creator: in man there shines forth a reflection of God himself....The life which God offers to man is a gift by which God shares something of himself with his creature.

Evangelium Vitae

The deliberate decision to deprive an innocent human being of his life is always morally evil and can never be licit either as an end in itself or as a means to a good end. It is in fact a grave act of disobedience to the moral law, and indeed to God himself, the author and guarantor of that law.

Evangelium Vitae

I do not hesitate to proclaim before you and before the world that all human life—from the moment of conception and through all subsequent stages—is sacred, because human life is created in the image and likeness of God. Nothing surpasses the greatness or dignity of a human person. Human life is not just an idea or an abstraction; human life is the concrete reality of a being that lives, that acts, that grows and develops; human life is the concrete reality of a being that is capable of love, and of service to humanity.…

Human life is precious because it is the gift of a God whose love is infinite; and when God gives life, it is forever.

HOMILY, CAPITOL MALL, WASHINGTON, D.C., 1979

All human beings ought to value every person for his or her uniqueness as a creature of God, called to be a brother or sister of Christ by reason of the Incarnation and the universal Redemption. For us, the sacredness of human life is based on these premises. And it is on these same premises that there is based our celebration of life—all human life. This explains our efforts to defend human life against every influence or action that threatens or weakens it, as well as our endeavors to make every life more human in all its aspects.

HOMILY, CAPITOL MALL, WASHINGTON, D.C., 1979

$\mathcal{T}$he human person is a unique composite—a unity of spirit and matter, soul and body, fashioned in the image of God and destined to live forever. Every human life is sacred, because every human person is sacred. It is in the light of this fundamental truth that the Church constantly proclaims and defends the dignity of human life from the moment of conception to the moment of natural death.

MESSAGE TO HEALTH WORKERS, PHOENIX, 1987

$\mathcal{T}$he Church counters the culture of death with the culture of love.

AD LIMINA APOSTOLORUM—
BISHOPS' CONFERENCE OF BRAZIL, 10

$\mathcal{L}$ife is entrusted to man as a treasure which must not be squandered, as a talent which must be used well. Man must render an account of it to his Master....

EVANGELIUM VITAE

*R*espect for life and for the dignity of the human person extends also to the rest of creation, which is called to join man in praising God.

"THE ECOLOGICAL CRISIS," 1990

MARRIAGE AND THE FAMILY

The witness to Christ of the entire Christian community has a greater impact than that of a single individual. How important, then, is the Gospel witness of every Christian community, but especially the most fundamental of them all, the Christian family. In the face of many common evils, the Christian family that truly lives the truth of the Gospel in love is most certainly a sign of contradiction; and at the same time it is a source of great hope for those who are eager to do good.

HOMILY AT SAN FRANCISCO, 1987

$\mathcal{M}$arriage, with its character as an
exclusive and permanent union, is sacred
because its origin is in God. Christians, in
receiving the sacrament of marriage, share in
God's creative plan and receive the graces they
need to carry out their mission of raising and
educating their children, and to respond to the
call to holiness. It is a union different from any
other sort of human society, for it is based on
the mutual giving and receiving of husband and
wife in order to become "one flesh" (Gn 2:24),
living in a community of life and love, the
vocation of which is to be a "sanctuary of life."
By their faithful and persevering union, the
couple contributes to the good of the
institution of the family and shows that a man
and a woman are capable of giving themselves
to one another forever....

HOMILY AT SANTA CLARA, CUBA, 1998

$\mathcal{C}$ontemporary society has a special need of
the witness of couples who persevere in their
union as an eloquent, even if sometimes
suffering, "sign" in our human condition of the
steadfastness of God's love. Day after day,
Christian married couples are called to open
their hearts ever more to the Holy Spirit,

whose power never fails and who enables them to love each other as Christ has loved us.

HOMILY AT COLUMBIA, SOUTH CAROLINA, 1987

𝒯he family is the first school of living, and the influence received inside the family is decisive for the future development of the individual.

MESSAGE FOR WORLD DAY OF PEACE, 1998

𝒜lthough people are rightly worried— though much less than they should be—about preserving the natural habitats of the various animal species threatened with extinction…too little effort is made to safeguard the moral conditions for an authentic "human ecology."…man too is God's gift to man. He must therefore respect the natural and moral structure with which he has been endowed.…

The first and fundamental structure for "human ecology" is the family, in which man receives his first formative ideas about truth and goodness, and learns what it means to love and to be loved, and thus what it actually means to be a person. Here we mean the family founded on marriage....

It is necessary to go back to seeing the family as the sanctuary of life. The family is indeed sacred: it is the place in which life—the gift of God—can be properly welcomed and protected against the many attacks to which it is exposed, and can develop in accordance with what constitutes authentic human growth. In the face of the so-called culture of death, the family is the heart of the culture of life.

Centesimus Annus

*T*he Church and the family are each in its own way living representations in human history of the eternal loving communion of the three persons of the Most Holy Trinity. In fact, the family is called the Church in miniature, "the domestic church," a particular expression of the Church through the human experience of love and common life. Like the Church, the family ought to be a place where the Gospel is transmitted and from which the Gospel radiates to other families and to the whole of society.

Homily at Columbia, South Carolina, 1987

Catholic parents must learn to form their family as a "domestic Church," a church in the home as it were, where God is honored, his law is respected, prayer is a normal event, virtue is transmitted by word and example, and everyone shares the hopes, the problems, and sufferings of everyone else.

HOMILY AT AQUEDUCT RACETRACK, 1995

The family is the first setting of evangelization, the place where the good news of Christ is first received and then, in simple yet profound ways, handed on from generation to generation.

MEETING WITH AFRICAN AMERICANS,
NEW ORLEANS, 1987

It is above all in the home that, before ever a word is spoken, children should experience God's love in the love which surrounds them. In the family they learn that God wants peace and mutual understanding among all human beings, who are called to be one great family.

MESSAGE FOR WORLD DAY OF PEACE, 1996

$\mathcal{L}$ord God, from you every family in heaven and on earth takes its name. Father, you are Love and Life.

Through your Son, Jesus Christ, born of woman, and through the Holy Spirit, the fountain of divine charity, grant that every family on earth may become for each successive generation a true shrine of life and love.

Grant that your grace may guide the thoughts and actions of husbands and wives for the good of their families and of all the families in the world.

Grant that the young may find in the family solid support for their human dignity and for their growth in truth and love.

Grant that love, strengthened by the grace of the sacrament of marriage, may prove mightier than all the weaknesses and trials through which our families sometimes pass.

Through the intercession of the Holy Family of Nazareth, grant that the Church may fruitfully carry out her worldwide mission in the family and through the family.

We ask this of you, who are Life, Truth, and Love with the Son and the Holy Spirit. Amen.

PRAYER FOR THE 1980 SYNOD OF BISHOPS

Solidarity and Human Relationships

Much to be envied are those who can give their lives for something greater than themselves in loving service to others. This, more than words or deeds alone, is what draws people to Christ.

Address at Carmel Mission, Monterey, 1987

$\mathcal{P}$eople need to be treated individually as persons, in the knowledge that Christ shed all his Precious Blood for each of them.

AD LIMINA APOSTOLORUM—
BISHOPS' CONFERENCE OF BRAZIL, 10

$\mathcal{T}$rue happiness lies in giving ourselves in love to our brothers and sisters.

MESSAGE TO YOUNG PEOPLE,
CAMAGÜEY, CUBA, 1998

$\mathcal{N}$o one can consider himself extraneous or indifferent to the lot of another member of the human family. No one can say that he is not responsible for the well-being of his brother or sister.

CENTESIMUS ANNUS

$\mathcal{E}$very man is his "brother's keeper," because God entrusts us to one another.

EVANGELIUM VITAE

$\mathcal{T}$he path of human solidarity is the path of service; and true service means selfless love, open to the needs of all, without distinction of persons, with the explicit purpose of reinforcing each person's sense of God-given dignity.

MEETING WITH CHARITIES, SAN ANTONIO, 1987

$\mathcal{S}$olidarity is not a feeling of vague compassion or shallow distress at the misfortunes of so many people, both near and far. On the contrary, it is a firm and persevering determination to commit oneself to the common good; that is to say to the good of all and of each individual, because we are all really responsible for all....

The exercise of solidarity within each society is valid when its members recognize one another as persons. Those who are more influential, because they have a greater share of goods and common services, should feel responsible for the weaker and be ready to share with them all they possess. Those who are weaker, for their part, in the same spirit of solidarity, should not adopt a purely passive attitude or one that is destructive of the social fabric, but, while claiming their legitimate rights, should do what they can for the good of all. The intermediate groups, in their turn, should not selfishly insist on their particular interests, but respect the interests of others.

Sollicitudo Rei Socialis

*T*he poor…are your brothers and sisters in Christ. You must never be content to leave them just the crumbs from the feast. You must take of your substance, and not just of your abundance, in order to help them. And you must treat them like guests at your family table.

Homily at Yankee Stadium, New York, 1979

*O*ther people are not rivals from whom we must defend ourselves, but brothers and sisters to be supported. They are to be loved for their own sakes, and they enrich us by their very presence.

Evangelium Vitae

$\mathcal{A}$ society of genuine solidarity can be built only if the well-off, in helping the poor, do not stop at giving from what they do not need. Moreover, offering material things is not enough: what is needed is a spirit of sharing, so that we consider it an honor to be able to devote our care and attention to the needs of our brothers and sisters in difficulty....Those living in poverty can wait no longer: they need help *now* and so have a right to receive *immediately* what they need.

MESSAGE FOR WORLD DAY OF PEACE, 1998

$\mathcal{M}$erciful love is absolutely necessary, in particular, for people who are close to one another: for husbands and wives, parents and children, and among friends....We must ask ourselves whether human relationships are being based, as they should be, on the merciful love and forgiveness revealed by God in Jesus Christ. We must examine our own heart and see how willing we are to forgive and to accept forgiveness in this world as well as in the next.

HOMILY AT NEW ORLEANS, 1987

*T*he more you cling to Jesus, the more capable you will become of being close to one another....

MESSAGE FOR WORLD YOUTH DAY, 1996

*K*eep Jesus Christ in your hearts, and you will recognize his face in every human being. You will want to help him out in all his needs: the needs of your brothers and sisters. This is the way we prepare ourselves to meet Jesus, when he will come again, on the last day, as the judge of the living and the dead....

ADDRESS, SHEA STADIUM, NEW YORK, 1979

*J*esus is living next to you, in the brothers and sisters with whom you share your daily existence. His visage is that of the poorest, of the marginalized who not infrequently are victims of an unjust model of development, in which profit is given first place and the human being is made a means rather than an end. Jesus' dwelling is wherever a human person is suffering because rights are denied, hopes betrayed, anxieties ignored. There, in the midst of humankind, is the dwelling of Christ, who asks you to dry every tear in his name, and to remind whoever feels lonely that no one whose hope is placed in him is ever alone.

MESSAGE FOR WORLD YOUTH DAY, 1996

*T*oday perhaps more than in the past, people are realizing that they are linked together by a common destiny, which is to be constructed together, if catastrophe for all is to be avoided…the good to which we are all called and the happiness to which we aspire cannot be obtained without an effort and commitment on the part of all, nobody excluded, and the consequent renouncing of personal selfishness.

SOLLICITUDO REI SOCIALIS

*I*t can hardly be hoped that children will one day be able to build a better world, unless there is a specific commitment to their education for peace. Children need to "learn peace": it is their right, and one which cannot be disregarded.

MESSAGE FOR WORLD DAY OF PEACE, 1996

$\mathcal{P}$eace is not a utopia, nor an inaccessible ideal, nor an unrealizable dream.

War is not an inevitable calamity.

Peace is possible.

And because it is possible, peace is our duty: our grave duty, our supreme responsibility.

Certainly peace is difficult; certainly it demands much good will, wisdom, and tenacity. But man can and he must make the force of reason prevail over the reasons of force....

And since peace, entrusted to the responsibility of men and women, remains even then a gift of God, it must also express itself in prayer to Him who holds the destinies of all peoples in His hands.

"NEGOTIATION," 1982

$\mathcal{S}$pirit of God, pour your light and your love into human hearts to achieve reconciliation between individuals, within families, between neighbors, in cities and villages, and within the institutions of civil society!

HOMILY AT THE NAVAL BASE ESPLANADE,
LEBANON, 1997

PROGRESS AND THE MODERN WORLD

Men and women are made in the image and likeness of God. So people may never be regarded as mere objects, nor may they be sacrificed for political, economic, or social gain. We must never allow them to be manipulated or enslaved by ideologies or technology. Their God-given dignity and worth as human beings forbid this.

GREETING TO U.N. STAFF, 1995

$\mathcal{M}$an lives at the same time both in the world of material values and in that of spiritual values. For the individual living and hoping man, his needs, freedoms, and relationships with others never concern one sphere of values alone, but belong to both.

ADDRESS TO U.N. GENERAL ASSEMBLY, 1979

$\mathcal{M}$odern man easily forgets the proportion, or rather, the lack of proportion between what he has received and what he is obliged to give. He has grown so much in his own eyes and is so sure that everything is the work of his own genius and of his own "industry," that he no longer sees the One who is the Alpha and the Omega, the Beginning and the End, the One who is the First Source of all that is as well as its Final End, the One in whom all that exists finds its proper meaning.

HOMILY AT NEW ORLEANS, 1987

$\mathcal{D}$emocracy cannot be idolized to the point of making it a substitute for morality or a panacea for immorality. Fundamentally, democracy is a "system" and as such is a means and not an end. Its "moral" value is not automatic, but depends on conformity to the moral law to which it, like every other form of human behavior, must be subject....

EVANGELIUM VITAE

*F*rom bitter experience, we know that the fear of "difference," especially when it expresses itself in a narrow and exclusive nationalism which denies any rights to "the other," can lead to a true nightmare of violence and terror. And yet if we make the effort to look at matters objectively, we can see that, transcending all the differences which distinguish individuals and peoples, there is a fundamental commonality. For different cultures are but different ways of facing the question of the meaning of personal existence....Every culture is an effort to ponder the mystery of the world and in particular of the human person: it is a way of giving expression to the transcendent dimension of human life. The heart of every culture is its approach to the greatest of all mysteries: the mystery of God.

Our respect for the culture of others is therefore rooted in our respect for each community's attempt to answer the question of human life....

To cut oneself off from the reality of difference—or, worse, to attempt to stamp out that difference—is to cut oneself off from the possibility of sounding the depths of the mystery of human life....The "difference" which some find so threatening can, through respectful dialogue, become the source of a deeper understanding of the mystery of human existence.

Address to U.N. General Assembly, 1995

*E*very person has the right to hear the "Good News" of the God who reveals and gives himself in Christ, so that each one can live out in its fullness his or her proper calling.

Redemptoris Missio

*W*hen the Church demands religious freedom she is not asking for a gift, a privilege, or a permission dependent on contingent situations, political strategies, or the will of the authorities. Rather, she demands the effective recognition of an inalienable human right....It is not simply a matter of a right belonging to the Church as an institution, it is also a matter of a right belonging to every person and every people. Every individual and every people will be spiritually enriched to the extent that religious freedom is acknowledged and put into practice.

MEETING WITH CUBAN BISHOPS, 1998

*R*eligious tolerance is based on the conviction that God wishes to be adored by people who are free: a conviction which requires us to respect and honor the inner sanctuary of conscience in which each person meets God.

GREETING IN BALTIMORE CATHEDRAL, 1995

*P*rogress usually tends to be measured according to the criteria of science and technology....Even so, this is not the only measure of progress, nor in fact is it the principal one. Much more important is the social and ethical dimension, which deals with human relations and spiritual values. In this area...society certainly owes much to the *"genius of women."*

LETTER TO WOMEN

*W*omanhood expresses the "human" as much as manhood does, but in a different and complementary way....It is only through the duality of the "masculine" and the "feminine" that the "human" finds full realization.

LETTER TO WOMEN

*T*he disabled person is one of us and participates fully in the same humanity that we possess. It would be radically unworthy of man, and a denial of our common humanity, to admit to the life of the community, and thus admit to work, only those who are fully functional. To do so would be to practice a serious form of discrimination, that of the strong and healthy against the weak and sick.

LABOREM EXERCENS

*H*owever true it may be that man is destined for work and called to it, in the first place work is "for man" and not man "for work."...in the final analysis it is always man who is the purpose of the work, whatever work it is that is done by man—even if the common

scale of values rates it as the merest "service,"
as the most monotonous, even the most
alienating work.

LABOREM EXERCENS

It is a strict duty of justice and truth not to
allow fundamental human needs to remain
unsatisfied, and not to allow those burdened by
such needs to perish.

CENTESIMUS ANNUS

When the scale of values is inverted and
politics, the economy, and social activity are no
longer placed at the service of people, the
human person comes to be viewed as a means
rather than respected as the center and end of
all these activities, and man is made to suffer in
his essence and in his transcendent dimension.
Human beings are then seen simply as
consumers, and freedom is understood in a very
individualistic and reductive sense, or men and
women are seen as mere producers with little
room for the exercise of civil and political
liberties. None of these social and political

models fosters a climate of openness to the transcendence of the person who freely seeks God.

MEETING WITH CUBAN BISHOPS, 1998

*J*ustice will never be fully attained unless people see in the poor person, who is asking for help in order to survive, not an annoyance or a burden, but an opportunity for showing kindness and a chance for greater enrichment. Only such an awareness can give the courage needed to face the risk and the change involved in every authentic attempt to come to the aid of another.

CENTESIMUS ANNUS

*L*et us work together so that everyone may have bread.

ADDRESS TO WORLD FOOD SUMMIT, 1996

*T*he poor have needs which are not only material and economic, but also involve liberating their potential to work out their own

destiny and to provide for the well-being of
their families and communities.

WELCOME ADDRESS, NEWARK
INTERNATIONAL AIRPORT, 1995

$\mathcal{I}$t is manifestly unjust that a privileged few
should continue to accumulate excess goods,
squandering available resources, while masses
of people are living in conditions of misery at
the very lowest level of subsistence. Today, the
dramatic threat of ecological breakdown is
teaching us the extent to which greed and
selfishness—both individual and collective—
are contrary to the order of creation, an order
which is characterized by mutual inter-
dependence.

"THE ECOLOGICAL CRISIS," 1990

$\mathcal{I}$t is not wrong to want to live better; what
is wrong is a style of life which is presumed to
be better when it is directed toward "having"
rather than "being," and which wants to have
more, not in order to be more but in order to
spend life in enjoyment as an end in itself. It is
therefore necessary to create lifestyles in which

the quest for truth, beauty, goodness and
communion with others for the sake of
common growth are the factors which
determine consumer choices, savings and
investments.

CENTESIMUS ANNUS

I wish to appeal with simplicity and
humility to everyone, to all men and women
without exception. I wish to ask them to be
convinced of the seriousness of the present
moment and of each one's individual
responsibility, and to implement—by the way
they live as individuals and as families, by the
use of their resources, by their civic activity, by
contributing to economic and political
decisions and by personal commitment to
national and international undertakings—the
measures inspired by solidarity and love of
preference for the poor.

SOLLICITUDO REI SOCIALIS

The poor ask for the right to share in
enjoying material goods and to make good use
of their capacity for work, thus creating a world

that is more just and prosperous for all. The advancement of the poor constitutes a great opportunity for the moral, cultural and even economic growth of all humanity.

CENTESIMUS ANNUS

The best kind of assistance is that which encourages the needy to become the primary artisans of their own social and cultural development.

CATHOLIC RELIEF SERVICES MESSAGE, 1995

Political leaders, and citizens of rich countries…especially if they are Christians, have the moral obligation, according to the degree of each one's responsibility, to take into consideration, in personal decisions and decisions of government,…this inter-dependence which exists between their conduct and the poverty and under-development of so many millions of people.

SOLLICITUDO REI SOCIALIS

$\mathcal{D}$evelopment must not be understood solely in economic terms, but in a way that is fully human. It is not only a question of raising all peoples to the level currently enjoyed by the richest countries, but rather of building up a more decent life through united labor, of concretely enhancing every individual's dignity and creativity, as well as his capacity to respond to his personal vocation, and thus to God's call. The apex of development is the exercise of the right and duty to seek God, to know him and to live in accordance with that knowledge.

CENTESIMUS ANNUS

$\mathcal{S}$ide-by-side with the miseries of underdevelopment, themselves unacceptable, we find ourselves up against a form of *superdevelopment*, equally inadmissible, because like the former it is contrary to what is good and to true happiness. This superdevelopment, which consists in an excessive availability of every kind of material goods for the benefit of certain social groups, easily makes people slaves of "possession" and of immediate gratification, with no other horizon than the multiplication or continual replacement of the things already owned with others still better. This is the so-called civilization of "consumption" or "consumerism," which involves so much "throwing-away" and "waste." An object already owned but now superseded by something better is discarded, with no thought of its possible lasting value in itself, nor of some other human being who is poorer.

All of us experience firsthand the sad effects of this blind submission to pure consumerism: in the first place a crass materialism, and at the same time a radical dissatisfaction, because one quickly learns—unless one is shielded from the flood of publicity and the ceaseless and tempting offers of products—that the more one possesses the more one wants, while deeper aspirations remain unsatisfied and perhaps even stifled.

Sollicitudo Rei Socialis

To "have" objects and goods does not in itself perfect the human subject, unless it contributes to the maturing and enrichment of that subject's "being," that is to say unless it contributes to the realization of the human vocation as such....

There are some people—the few who possess much—who do not really succeed in "being" because, through a reversal of the hierarchy of values, they are hindered by the cult of "having"; and there are others—the many who have little or nothing—who do not succeed in realizing their basic human vocation because they are deprived of essential goods.

The evil does not consist in "having" as such, but in possessing without regard for the quality and the ordered hierarchy of the goods one has. Quality and hierarchy arise from the subordination of goods and their availability to man's "being" and his true vocation.

SOLLICITUDO REI SOCIALIS

*P*art of the teaching and most ancient practice of the Church is her conviction that she is obliged by her vocation—she herself, her ministers and each of her members—to relieve the misery of the suffering, both far and near, not only out of her "abundance" but also out of her "necessities." Faced by cases of need, one cannot ignore them in favor of superfluous church ornaments and costly furnishings for divine worship; on the contrary it could be obligatory to sell these goods in order to provide food, drink, clothing and shelter for those who lack these things....here we are shown a "hierarchy of values"...between "having" and "being," especially when the "having" of a few can be to the detriment of the "being" of many others.

SOLLICITUDO REI SOCIALIS

$\mathcal{T}$he best legacy you can leave to future generations will be to pass on the higher values of the Spirit. It is not a matter of merely preserving some of these, but rather of promoting an ethical and civic training which will help people to accept new values and to reshape their own character and the heart of society on the basis of an education for freedom, social justice, and responsibility.

MESSAGE TO YOUNG PEOPLE, CAMAGÜEY, CUBA, 1998

$\mathcal{S}$ocial injustice and unjust social structures exist only because individuals and groups of individuals deliberately maintain or tolerate them. It is these personal choices, operating through structures, that breed and propagate situations of poverty, oppression, and misery. For this reason, overcoming "social" sin and reforming the social order itself must begin with the conversion of our hearts.

MEETING WITH CHARITIES, SAN ANTONIO, 1987

The purpose of a business firm is not simply to make a profit, but is to be found in its very existence as a community of persons who in various ways are endeavoring to satisfy their basic needs, and who form a particular group at the service of the whole of society. Profit is a regulator of the life of a business, but it is not the only one; other human and moral factors must also be considered which, in the long term, are at least equally important for the life of a business.

CENTESIMUS ANNUS

When man turns his back on the Creator's plan, he provokes a disorder which has inevitable repercussions on the rest of the created order. If man is not at peace with God, then earth itself cannot be at peace.

"THE ECOLOGICAL CRISIS," 1990

When man disobeys God and refuses to submit to his rule, nature rebels against him and no longer recognizes him as its "master," for he has tarnished the divine image in himself. The claim to ownership and use of created things remains still valid, but after sin its exercise becomes difficult and full of suffering.

SOLLICITUDO REI SOCIALIS

The dominion granted to man by the Creator is not an absolute power, nor can one speak of a freedom to "use and misuse," or to dispose of things as one pleases. The limitation imposed from the beginning by the Creator himself and expressed symbolically by the prohibition not to "eat of the fruit of the tree" shows clearly enough that, when it comes to the natural world, we are subject not only to biological laws but also to moral ones, which cannot be violated with impunity.

SOLLICITUDO REI SOCIALIS

$\mathcal{W}$e must not be afraid of the future. We must not be afraid of man. It is no accident that we are here. Each and every human person has been created in the "image and likeness" of the One who is the origin of all that is. We have within us the capacities for wisdom and virtue. With these gifts, and with the help of God's grace, we can build in the next century and the next millennium a civilization worthy of the human person, a true culture of freedom. We can and must do so! And in doing so, we shall see that the tears of this century have prepared the ground for a new springtime of the human spirit.

ADDRESS TO U.N. GENERAL ASSEMBLY, 1995

THE CHURCH

*The Church's fundamental function
in every age and particularly in ours is to
direct man's gaze, to point the awareness and
experience of the whole of humanity toward
the mystery of Christ, to help all men to be
familiar with the profundity of the
Redemption taking place in Christ Jesus.*

REDEMPTOR HOMINIS

$\mathcal{T}$he Church wishes to serve this single end: that each person may be able to find Christ, in order that Christ may walk with each person....

REDEMPTOR HOMINIS

$\mathcal{T}$he Church is catholic...because she is able to present in every human context the revealed truth, preserved by her intact in its divine content, in such a way as to bring it into contact with the lofty thoughts and just expectations of every individual and every people.

SLAVORUM APOSTOLI

$\mathcal{T}$he Church has endured for 2000 years. Like the mustard seed in the Gospel, she has grown and become a great tree, able to cover the whole of humanity with her branches.

TERTIO MILLENNIO ADVENIENTE

The Gospel of Jesus Christ, which is the great gift of God's love, is never in contrast with what is noble and pure in the life of any tribe or nation, since all good things are his gifts.

MEETING WITH NATIVE AMERICANS, PHOENIX, 1987

In the Church there are many different gifts. There is room for many different cultures and ways of doing things. But there is no room in the Church for selfishness.

MEETING WITH YOUTH, NEW ORLEANS, 1987

Salvation, which comes as a free gift of divine love in Christ, is not offered to us on a purely individual basis. It comes to us through and in the Church. Through our communion with Christ and with one another on earth, we are given a foretaste of that perfect communion reserved for heaven. Our communion is also meant to be a sign or sacrament which draws other people to Christ, so that all might be saved.

MEETING WITH LAITY, SAN FRANCISCO, 1987

$\mathcal{T}$he unity of all divided humanity is the will of God....On the eve of his sacrifice on the Cross, Jesus himself prayed to the Father for his disciples and for all those who believe in him, that they might be one, a living communion....How is it possible to remain divided, if we have been "buried" through Baptism in the Lord's death, in the very act by which God, through the death of his Son, has broken down the walls of division?

ET UNUM SINT

$\mathcal{E}$cumenism, the movement promoting Christian unity, is not just some sort of "appendix" which is added to the Church's traditional activity. Rather, ecumenism is an organic part of her life and work, and consequently must pervade all that she is and does; it must be like the fruit borne by a healthy and flourishing tree which grows to its full stature.

ET UNUM SINT

*L*et us make no mistake about it: as if by some evangelical instinct, the humble and simple faithful spontaneously sense when the Gospel is being served in the Church and when it is eviscerated and asphyxiated by other interests.

OPENING ADDRESS, PUEBLA CONFERENCE, 1979

*I*f there is one challenge facing the Church and her priests today, it is the challenge of transmitting the Christian message whole and entire, without letting it be emptied of its substance. The Gospel cannot be reduced to mere human wisdom. Salvation lies not in clever human words or schemes, but in the Cross and Resurrection of our Lord Jesus Christ.

ADDRESS AT VESPERS, ST. JOSEPH'S SEMINARY, 1995

THE SACRAMENTS

In Christ, the Holy Spirit makes us God's beloved children. The Incarnation of the Son of God happened once, and is unrepeatable. Divine adoption goes on all the time, through the Church, the Body of Christ, and particularly through the Sacraments, through Baptism, Penance, the Eucharist, and of course the Sacrament of Pentecost that we call Confirmation.

HOMILY AT CENTRAL PARK, 1995

On the day of our Baptism, we received the greatest gift God can bestow on any man or woman. No other honor, no other distinction will equal its value. For we were freed from sin and incorporated into Christ Jesus and his Body, the Church.

MESSAGE TO RELIGIOUS WOMEN,
WASHINGTON, D.C., 1979

Baptism is not simply a seal of conversion, a kind of external sign....Rather, it is the sacrament which signifies and effects rebirth from the Spirit, establishes real and unbreakable bonds with the Blessed Trinity, and makes us members of the Body of Christ, which is the Church.

REDEMPTORIS MISSIO

Confession is an act of honesty and courage; an act of entrusting ourselves, beyond sin, to the mercy of a loving and forgiving God. It is an act of the prodigal son who returns to his Father and is welcomed by him with the kiss of peace.

HOMILY AT SAN ANTONIO, 1987

$\mathcal{I}$t is a mark of greatness to be able to say: "I have made a mistake; I have sinned, Father; I have offended you, my God; I am sorry; I ask for pardon; I will try again because I rely on your strength and I believe in your love. And I know that the power of your Son's paschal mystery—the death and resurrection of our Lord Jesus Christ—is greater than my weaknesses and all the sins of the world. I will come and confess my sins and be healed, and I will live in your love!"

HOMILY AT SAN ANTONIO, 1987

$\mathcal{I}$n faithfully observing the centuries-old practice of the Sacrament of Penance—the practice of individual confession with a personal act of sorrow and the intention to amend and make satisfaction—the Church is therefore defending the human soul's individual right: man's right to a more personal encounter with the crucified forgiving Christ, with Christ saying, through the minister of the Sacrament of Reconciliation: "Your sins are forgiven" (Mk 2:5); "Go, and do not sin again" (Jn 8:11). As is evident, this is also a right on Christ's part with regard to every human being redeemed by him:

his right to meet each one of us in that key
moment in the soul's life constituted by the
moment of conversion and forgiveness.

REDEMPTOR HOMINIS

*I*n our celebration of the Word of God, the
mystery of Christ opens up before us and
envelops us. And through union with our
Head, Jesus Christ, we become ever more
increasingly one with all the members of his
Body. As never before, it becomes possible for
us to reach out and embrace the world, but to
embrace it with Christ: with authentic
generosity, with pure and effective love, in
service, in healing, and in reconciliation.

MORNING PRAYER, ST. PATRICK'S CATHEDRAL, 1979

*I*n the Eucharist, the Son, who is of one
being with the Father, the One whom only the
Father knows, offers himself in sacrifice to the
Father for humanity and for all creation. In the
Eucharist Christ gives back to the Father
everything that has come from him. Thus there
is brought about a profound *mystery of justice on
the part of the creature towards the Creator*. Man

needs to honor his Creator by offering to him, in an act of thanksgiving and praise, all that he has received. *Man must never lose sight of this debt,* which he alone, among all other earthly realities, is capable of acknowledging and paying back as the one creature made in God's own image and likeness. At the same time, given his creaturely limitations and sinful condition, man would be incapable of making this act of justice towards the Creator, had not Christ himself, the Son who is of one being with the Father and also true man, first given us the Eucharist.

GIFT AND MYSTERY

The Eucharist…shows us…what value each person, our brother or sister, has in God's eyes, if Christ offers himself equally to each one, under the species of bread and wine. If our Eucharistic worship is authentic, it must make us grow in awareness of the dignity of each person.…

Christ comes into the hearts of our brothers and sisters and visits their consciences. How the image of each and every one changes, when we become aware of this reality, when we make it the subject of our reflections!

DOMINICAE CENAE

*E*ucharistic worship is not so much worship of the inaccessible transcendence as worship of the divine condescension, and it is also the merciful and redeeming transformation of the world in the human heart.

DOMINICAE CENAE

THE PRIESTHOOD

*If we take a close look at what contemporary
men and women expect from priests, we will
see that, in the end, they have but one great
expectation: they are thirsting for Christ.
Everything else—their economic, social,
and political needs—can be met by any
number of other people. From the priest they
ask for Christ! And from him they have the
right to receive Christ, above all through the
proclamation of the word.*

GIFT AND MYSTERY

I am convinced that a priest…should… have no fear of being "behind the times," because the human "today" of every priest is included in the "today" of Christ the Redeemer. For every priest, in every age, the greatest task is each day to discover his own priestly "today" in the "today" of Christ….

GIFT AND MYSTERY

*W*hat does it mean to be a priest? According to Saint Paul, it means above all to be *a steward of the mysteries of God*….The steward is not the owner, but the one to whom the owner entrusts his goods so that he will manage them justly and responsibly. In exactly the same way the priest receives from Christ the treasures of salvation, in order duly to distribute them among the people to whom he is sent. These treasures are those of faith….No one may consider himself the "owner" of these treasures; they are meant for us all. But, by reason of what Christ laid down, the priest has the task of administering them.

GIFT AND MYSTERY

Christ needs holy priests! Today's world demands holy priests! Only a holy priest can become, in an increasingly secularized world, a resounding witness to Christ and his Gospel. And only thus can a priest become a guide for men and women and a teacher of holiness. People, especially the young, are looking for such guides. A priest can be a guide and teacher only to the extent that he becomes an authentic witness!

GIFT AND MYSTERY

If Christ—by his free and sovereign choice, clearly attested to by the Gospel and by the Church's constant Tradition—entrusted only to men the task of being an "icon" of his countenance as "shepherd" and "bridegroom" of the Church through the exercise of the ministerial priesthood, this in no way detracts from the role of women, or for that matter from the role of the other members of the Church who are not ordained to the sacred ministry, since *all* share equally in the dignity proper to the "common priesthood" based on Baptism.

These role distinctions should not be viewed in accordance with the criteria of functionality typical in human societies. Rather they must be understood according to the particular criteria of the *sacramental economy*, i.e., the economy of "signs" which God freely chooses in order to become present in the midst of humanity.

LETTER TO WOMEN

MARY

Like Mary, you must not be afraid to allow the Holy Spirit to help you become intimate friends of Christ. Like Mary, you must put aside any fear, in order to take Christ to the world in whatever you do—in marriage, as single people in the world, as students, as workers, as professional people. Christ wants to go to many places in the world, and to enter many hearts, through you. Just as Mary visited Elizabeth, so you too are called to "visit" the needs of the poor, the hungry, the homeless, those who are alone or ill. . . .

Homily at Central Park, 1995

$\mathcal{T}$his woman of faith, Mary of Nazareth, the Mother of God, has been given to us as a model in our pilgrimage of faith. From Mary we learn to surrender to God's will in all things. From Mary, we learn to trust even when all hope seems gone. From Mary, we learn to love Christ, her Son and the Son of God. For Mary is not only the Mother of God, she is Mother of the Church as well.

MESSAGE TO PRIESTS, WASHINGTON, D.C., 1979

$\mathcal{A}$t Cana in Galilee there is shown only one concrete aspect of human need, apparently a small one and of little importance ("They have no wine"). But it has a symbolic value: this coming to the aid of human needs means, at the same time, bringing those needs within the radius of Christ's messianic mission and salvific power. Thus there is a mediation: Mary places herself between her Son and mankind in the reality of their wants, needs and sufferings. She puts herself "in the middle," that is to say she acts as a mediatrix not as an outsider, but in her position as mother. She knows that as such she can point out to her son the needs of mankind, and in fact, she "has the right" to do so. Her mediation is thus in the nature of intercession: Mary "intercedes" for mankind. And that is not all. As a mother she also wishes the messianic power of her son to be manifested, that salvific power of his which is meant to help man in his misfortunes, to free him from the evil which in various forms and degrees weighs heavily upon his life....

Another essential element of Mary's maternal task is found in her words to the servants: "Do whatever he tells you." The Mother of Christ presents herself as the spokeswoman of her Son's will, pointing out those things which must be done so that the salvific power of the Messiah may be manifested. At Cana, thanks to the intercession of Mary and the obedience of the servants, Jesus begins "his hour."

REDEMPTORIS MATER

O blessed Virgin, Mother of God, Mother of Christ, Mother of the Church, look upon us mercifully at this hour!

Virgo fidelis, faithful Virgin, pray for us! Teach us to believe as you believed! Make our faith in God, in Christ, in the Church, always to be limpid, serene, courageous, strong and generous.

Mater amabilis, Mother worthy of love! Mater pulchrae dilectionis, Mother of fair love, pray for us! Teach us to love God and our brothers, as you loved them: make our love for others to be always patient, kindly, respectful.

Causa nostrae laetitiae, Cause of our joy, pray for us! Teach us to be able to grasp, in faith, the paradox of Christian joy, which springs up and blooms from sorrow, renunciation, and union with your sacrificed Son: make our joy to be always genuine and full, in order to be able to communicate it to all! Amen.

PRAYER AT LOURDES GROTTO, VATICAN GARDENS, 1979

$\mathcal{I}$ leave you now with this prayer: that the Lord Jesus will reveal himself to each one of you, that he will give you the strength to go out and profess that you are Christian, that he will show you that he alone can fill your hearts. Accept his freedom and embrace his truth, and be messengers of the certainty that you have been truly liberated through the death and Resurrection of the Lord Jesus. This will be the new experience, the powerful experience, that will generate, through you, a more just society and a better world.

God bless you and may the joy of Jesus be always with you!

MESSAGE TO STUDENTS,
THE CATHOLIC UNIVERSITY, 1979

$\mathcal{P}$ERMISSIONS AND ACKNOWLEDGMENTS

The compiler wishes to express his gratitude to the following for granting permission to reproduce material of which they are the publisher or copyright holder:

Selections from *Crossing the Threshold of Hope* by His Holiness Pope John Paul II: Translation copyright © 1994 by Alfred A. Knopf, Inc. Reprinted by permission of the publisher.

Selections from *Centesimus Annus*, *Dives in Misericordia*, *Dominicae Cenae*, *Dominum et Vivificantem*, *Et Unum Sint*, *Evangelium Vitae*, *Laborem Exercens*, *Letter of the Pope to the Children in the Year of the Family*, *Letter to Women*, *Redemptor Hominis*, *Redemptoris Mater*, *Redemptoris Missio*, *Salvifici Doloris*, *Slavorum Apostoli*, *Sollicitudo Rei Socialis*, *Tertio Millennio Adveniente*, and *Veritatis Splendor* are reprinted by permission of Libreria Editrice Vaticana, 00120 Città del Vaticano.

Selections from the Holy Father's speeches, homilies, addresses, prayers, and greetings are reprinted by permission of *L' Osservatore Romano*.

Photos

page ii: Pope John Paul hugs two children upon his arrival in Baltimore, Maryland, in 1995. *(CNS photo)*

page v: Pope John Paul II pauses to pray at the National Shrine of the Basilica of the Assumption in Baltimore, 1995. *(CNS photo by Michael Okoniewski)*

page 113: Pope John Paul II distributes Communion at the Mass for World Youth Day, 1989. *(CNS photo by Arturo Mari)*